YOUR BEST IS NEXT

How to
Live Your
FULLEST LIFE
During Your
"Gun Lap"

IRA BLUMENTHAL

simple truths
Small books. BIG IMPACT.

Photo Credits
Internal images © page vi, xiii, 2, 30, 36, 70, 82, 97, Hero Images/Getty Images; page vi, joelblit/Getty Images; page vii, 20, 40, Peathegee Inc/Getty Images; page vii, 51, Cecilie_Arcurs/Getty Images; page xvi, Caiaimage/Sam Edwards/Getty Images; page 4, TVP Inc/Getty Images; page 10, Ozgur Donmaz/Getty Images, Taiyou Nomachi/Getty Images; page 12, Caiaimage/Agnieszka Olek/Getty Images; page 16, Sidekick/Getty Images; page 22, kali9/Getty Images; page 26, AfricaImages/Getty Images; page 38, Paul Bradbury/Getty Images, Tom Merton/Getty Images; page 42, Kazuko Kimizuka/Getty Images; page 52, Pavliha/Getty Images; page 60, Ariel Skelley/Getty Images; page 65, Artur Debat/Getty Images; page 66, Halfpoint/Getty Images; page 72, Pauline St.Denis/Getty Images; page 80, Jon Feingersh Photography Inc/Getty Images; page 92, Ronnie Kaufman/Getty Images; page 97, Nastasic/Getty Images; page 99, Colin Anderson Productions Pty Ltd/Getty Images; page 100, Darryl Leniuk/Getty Images; page 103, Shestock/Getty Images; page 105, Mint Images/Getty Images; page 108, Image Source/Getty Images; page 110, Alistair Berg/Getty Images

Internal images on pages iv, xi, xvi, 19, 35, 45, 46, 54, 66, 74, 78, 86, 88, 91, 98 have been provided by Pexels and Pixabay; these images are licensed under CC0 Creative Commons and have been released by the author for public use.

Published by Simple Truths, an imprint of Sourcebooks, Inc.
P.O. Box 4410, Naperville, Illinois 60567-4410
(630) 961-3900
Fax: (630) 961-2168
sourcebooks.com

Printed and bound in China.
OGP 10 9 8 7 6 5 4 3 2 1

I dedicate this book to the love of my life, my best friend, and surely the "wind beneath my wings," my dear wife, Kimberly Lain. I also dedicate this book to all those who have continually advised me to slow down. They were all unsuccessful in their counsel, but I am eternally grateful for their caring. Although they still don't accept that seventy is my middle age, my hope for them is they, too, one day discover the joy one can receive speeding up on the gun lap.

CONTENTS

INTRODUCTION

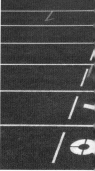

The Gun Lap

➡️ *It's not how well you start. What matters is how well you finish.*

The gun lap is the last lap of a race in which a pistol is fired as the racer in first place completes the penultimate lap. This immediately causes a surge in adrenaline, and even though the racer is in more pain than most people can imagine, he or she immediately picks up the pace and goes for a **strong finish**. It is also the signal to all the other runners that if they are to make progress and win or place, they need to move into sprint mode inasmuch as the finish (end) is near, clearly

understanding that **success in any race, or in any endeavor, at any age or stage, and certainly in life itself, is all about how one finishes.**

First used in 1939, the **gun lap** was a fixture of the track world for decades until the early 1970s, when a few public-interest groups lobbied to change what they thought to be a violent image (i.e., a gun) to a more peaceful ringing of a bell. Hence, today this lap is called *the bell lap*. Nonetheless, the message is clear. **Gun or bell, this signifies the finish is near.**

The concept of applying the gun lap to life is a simple, logical one. As we approach new phases in life (e.g., a milestone birthday, retirement, or any dramatic change), we all come to grips with the reality of both the closing of one chapter and the opening of another, and we all must face the challenges of change, even our own mortality. The gun lap is a metaphor that there is an end, whether it's in sight or many miles (years, decades) down the road. It's our wake-up call that reminds us **life's only regrets are typically related to the things we didn't do or didn't try to do.**

Obviously, work on new goals, new ambitions, and new personal quests can be exhausting. When you feel like stopping, think about why you started and revisit your initial goals. **Accomplishing even the smallest objectives can be empowering, exciting, exhilarating, and hugely satisfying.**

If you accept that **too late comes too soon** and convince yourself that for some activities there might not be a next time nor a second chance, you will stop putting things off and energetically put things on! As the saying goes, **"It's not the years in your life that count. It's the life in your years."** The gun lap makes us realize again and again **minutes are more important than money,** and we need to spend them wisely.

You might conclude that racing in the gun lap is likened to a second chance and ask the proverbial question, **"What's so important about a second chance?"** The answer is simple: **Everything!** Second chances, trying new activities, and seeking new ventures and adventures force us to learn new things, to master new skills, to focus on new goals, and to move forward in our life's journey. After all, trying something new or retrying something you've not done in a while writes a new and exciting chapter in your life's book.

Don't be distracted by age. Age is truly just a number. Don't let it define you. Be positive. Zig Ziglar said, "It's your attitude and not your aptitude that determines your altitude."

Age is an artificial barrier that too many people use to put limitations on their brain. When one considers the massive list of achievements done by individuals who ignored their age and focused on achieving, producing, and creating, you should be motivated and inspired to do the same in your life.

To put it another way, **"Age is an issue of mind over matter. If you don't mind, it doesn't matter."**

Whether it's taking up a new hobby, committing to a personal bucket list item, revitalizing a relationship, reinvigorating an old vocation, recalibrating one's life, finally taking that dream vacation, or starting a new career, **fulfilling lives are those that keep moving forward,** keep dreaming, and intently (and intentionally) focus on an ongoing commitment to productivity, progress, and achievement.

Regardless of your age and life stage, the gun lap metaphor is a signal to you that time is running out and you need to **focus on your finish.** Some of you see the gun lap (or the bell lap) as a wake-up call and face the last lap with great excitement and what has been called a runner's high. Still others become panicked and fearful of what lies ahead. Their fear is often focused on the unknown. Yet just as anyone who has had the unfortunate experience of being chased by a dog knows, **fear can be an amazing motivator**. Imagine how many Olympic records would be broken if every sprinter had a vicious Doberman pinscher behind a starting block ready to chase the runner when the starter pistol was fired.

Every one of us has dreams, aspirations, a bucket list, and plans to do something, visit someplace, and subtly—or blatantly—change who we are and what we do. **Everything in business and life is five percent ideas and ninety-five percent work and execution**. Most of us live in the five percent. We have no shortage of ideas. Sadly, hope has escaped many of us, and dreams have been forgotten. Facing your gun lap boldly and excitedly will motivate you to bring a project to closure, to fulfill a dream, and to be proud of realizing an important life purpose.

Ah, the search for your individual life's purposes is vital. The realization, then achievement, of that purpose is called *fulfillment*.

My single favorite saying is **"the two most important days in your life are the day you were born and the day you found out why."** Call it your *why* or your *purpose*, it's the very same thing.

As André Maurois said, "**Growing old is no more than a bad habit which a busy man has no time to form**." The real achievers in life understand it's not how old you are but, more importantly, *how you are old*.

Acknowledging and respecting all the gun lap represents will lead you to be goal-oriented, focused, and productive and revitalize your life with yet another new purpose.

This is all about life fulfillment.

CHAPTER ONE

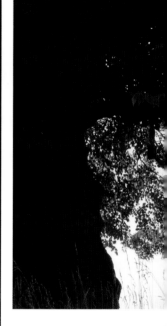

Walking the Talk

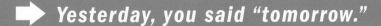 *Yesterday, you said "tomorrow."*

We've all heard the expression **talk is cheap.** That simply means talk is easy and very often has little value. Don't talk about it, be about it. Someone once said that God gave us two ears and one mouth and we should use them in that proportion. Sometimes, we talk far more than we listen (and act). People get a mental block, and I've heard of writer's block, but I've yet to hear of anyone getting a talker's block.

Nonetheless, talking about our plans, hopes, dreams, wishes, prayers, desires, goals, and aspirations is

simple. It's a no-brainer to have an idea, a hope, and a dream. Having these aspirations as something to strive for is what life is all about. Sadly, hopes and dreams and even plans are inactive and passive. **It's the chase, the hunt, the quest, the pursuit that's more important, because where hopes, dreams, and plans are passive...pursuit is active.**

We've all heard expressions such as **"all talk and no action," "actions speak louder than words," "you are what you do, not what you say you'll do,"** and **"actions always beat intention."** They all, painfully, mean the same thing.

An **invaluable key to success is action**. Former U.S. president Harry Truman had a sign on his desk that read "I'm from Missouri," a shortened form of the unofficial state motto, "I am from Missouri. You have got to show me."

Truman was about action and energy. On the campaign trail in 1948, a supporter yelled, "Give 'em hell, Harry!" That became a slogan forever attached to Truman. He wasn't about talking. He was about action and walking the talk.

IRA BLUMENTHAL

Personally, I'm a poster child for procrastination. I'm certainly not proud of that and need to improve in that area. Although I like to think we all procrastinate, I'm clearly one of the global leaders in the activity (or inactivity). I had to laugh out loud one day when I was walking in a conference center of a hotel and saw a sign on a workshop room that read, **"The Procrastinator Club's Meeting Has Been Postponed."**

We all talk the talk but seem too often plagued with a case of procrastination. I've read so many Mark Twain books and used his quotations so often that I see him as a personal friend, and so, to share one of my favorite Twain quotes: **"Never put off till tomorrow what you can do the day after tomorrow just as well."** Does that sound familiar? The truth always hurts.

Many years ago, I talked and talked and talked about the book I was writing. Truth be told, I was talking much more about the book than writing it. I was continuously drinking procrastinator's poison and realized, as we all inevitably do, that talking was far easier than walking.

One day, my son, Eric, who was nine years old at the time, came to me for one of those father-to-son, heart-to-heart talks. This time, it was more a son-to-father talk. He said something to the effect of, "**Dad, I've got to be honest with you**. The whole family is getting really tired of hearing you talk and talk and talk about the book you're writing. You've been talking about it for years. Mom told me that you've actually been talking about it for seven years. **Dad, either write it or don't write it.** Talking about it is really boring and painful."

He gave me a quotation he found that, decades later, still sits prominently on a wall near my desk. It's a quote from Mary Heaton Vorse, who told the writer Sinclair Lewis that **"the art of writing is the art of applying the seat of the pants to the seat of the chair."**

I was embarrassed. I was taken aback. I became motivated. I wrote and finished that book in three months. I applied the seat of my pants to my desk chair. The book went on to be highly acclaimed and successful. I owe it all to the wisdom of a nine-year-old. To this day, when someone asks me how long it took to write that book, I always answer "a little over seven years." They then typically say, **"Wow, seven years. You really worked hard on that book."** I reply, **"Actually, it took me nearly seven years talking about the book and three months writing it!"**

Although a history-making, iconic, upbeat painter, Picasso often tended to make what seemed to be dour, dismal, and dark statements about his viewpoints on life. One of those statements truthfully and sadly is a painful reality: **"Only put off until tomorrow what you are willing to die having left undone."**

We all talk about a book we plan on writing. We all talk about a patio or new deck or bookshelf we plan on building. We all talk about a new skill we plan on mastering. We all talk about plans (and hopes, aspirations, dreams) we have for the future.

The future comes upon us very quickly, and opportunities pass us by faster than cars racing on the highway.

If you procrastinate and wait for what we've all referred to as the perfect moment, that perfect moment will invariably pass you by. Focus on your objective and, as a Nike slogan reads, "Just Do It." Don't make excuses.

We've all delayed decisions, deferred choices, and tabled opportunities, even though we openly talked as if we were in hot pursuit of an opportunity. I'm not concerned with being repetitive: We must *stop* delaying and deferring. We must *start* doing.

Walk the talk. Walk the talk!

It's a simple game plan. Be positive. Say yes to opportunities. Believe in yourself. Follow through, do what you say you'll do, and don't wait for the perfect moment. **Every moment you're blessed with on this Earth is, in fact, the perfect moment for action and activity.**

CHAPTER TWO

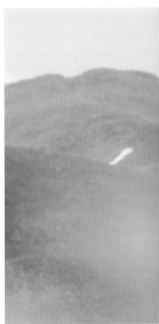

Everyone Has to Get Older

➡️ *Everyone has to get older. That doesn't mean you have to be old.*

Okay, you're getting older. My children would respond to that statement with "Duh!" It's a reality. It's not new. People have gotten older before. You're not the first, and you won't be the last, but you should **try with all your might to be the best!**

Sadly, the current correlation between aging and productivity is that too many people deceive themselves into

believing a blatant myth. They obsess that as they grow older, they have less energy, less propensity for creativity, less of an inclination to be open-minded, and less of a penchant for productivity. This negative viewpoint relating to your ability to envision, shape, build, create, generate, design, and implement is fueled by being surrounded by peers (yes, your family, friends, and coworkers) all believing in the same sad paradigm. You're never too old to learn, grow, prosper, and thrive.

What they see is what they'll be.

After all, age is just a number. Old age isn't defined as the end of the road. It's simply a road marker. Many great works of art, industry, and science came from individuals who society defined as old. Consider the following short list. If this isn't a motivator, close this book and go back to watching television.

- **JULIA CHILDS** debuted her first TV show, *The French Chef*, at age fifty-one.

- **NELSON MANDELA** became president of South Africa at age seventy-four.

- **BENJAMIN FRANKLIN** signed the Declaration of Independence at age seventy, became the chief executive of the state of Pennsylvania at age seventy-nine, and coauthored the U.S. Constitution at age eighty-one.

- **THURGOOD MARSHALL** became the first African American Supreme Court Justice at age fifty-nine.

- **MICHELANGELO** created the architectural plans for the Church of Santa Maria degli Angeli at the age of eighty-eight.

- **TONI MORRISON** was the first African American woman to win the Nobel Prize for Literature at the age of sixty-two.

- **PABLO PICASSO** completed his masterpiece, *Guernica*, at age fifty-five.

- **ANNA MARY ROBERTSON MOSES**, a.k.a. Grandma Moses, one of the biggest names in American folk art, started painting at seventy-six.

- **HARLAN SANDERS**, better known as Colonel Sanders, founded Kentucky Fried Chicken (KFC) at age sixty-five.

- **SOPHOCLES** wrote *Oedipus Rex* when he was seventy and *Electra* when he was eighty.

- **J. R. R. TOLKIEN** published the first volume of his classic fantasy series, The Lord of the Rings, at age sixty-two.

- **STEVEN TYLER**, Rock & Roll Hall of Famer and lead singer of Aerosmith, started a new career as a solo country singer at age sixty-eight and had a *Billboard* Country number one hit.

- **CORNELIUS VANDERBILT** started buying railroads at age seventy.

- **GUISEPPE VERDI** composed *Otello* when he was seventy-four and *Falstaff* at eighty.

- **NOAH WEBSTER** completed his monumental *American Dictionary of the English Language* at sixty-six.

- **LAURA INGALLS WILDER** completed her classic book *Little House on the Prairie* when she was seventy. (Her first book wasn't published until she was sixty-five.)

And the impressive list of gun-lap achievements goes on and on...

It's illogical to assume that great accomplishments can only be achieved by young people. After all, the young have fewer life experiences, a much smaller network for much-needed access, a limited time frame of references, and a smaller stash of readily available resources. **Sadly, the older you get, the more convinced you become of your inadequacies, inabilities, and inefficiencies.**

It's not about physical strength. **It's all about mental strength.** The very realism that comes with age becomes an inhibitor to visioning and dreaming.

Those who continue to work and avoid retirement in favor of recalibration are the happiest and most fulfilled. **You don't stop playing because you've grown old.** You grow old because you've stopped playing and working.

IRAs (a savings vehicle, no author pun intended), 401Ks, retirement plans, and other future-oriented, security-focused financial devices have all contributed to a society filled with baby boomers and Gen Xers slowly but surely cashing out and focusing on their next life (i.e., life after life). **However, cashing out doesn't have to mean checking out.**

Some people believe life begins at fifty, sixty, sixty-five, seventy, seventy-five, or even older. More people should take that attitude. After all, you're only as old as you feel and act. However, believing in the fountain of youth and finding that fountain are two very different activities. Just believing and wanting to stay young and vibrant is a proven waste of time. It's got to be more than just believing and wanting. Working, committing, and dedicating oneself to thinking young, acting young, and seeing the world through the eyes of wisdom but the heart of youth is a different drill.

As mentioned previously, pursuit is the key. Pursue being as active as you can. Pursue being surrounded by young people and young ideas. Pursue living your life with energy, spirit, and passion, which will all help you stay forever young.

CHAPTER THREE

Where (and Who) Are You Now?

 *Mirror, mirror on the wall.*

A memorable line from the Brothers Grimm fairy tale "Little Snow-White" was "mirror, mirror on the wall, who in this land is fairest of all?" As you get poised, prepared, and ready to race on your personal, important gun lap, you need to take stock. **You need to fully define (and come to reality with) the who, what, and where of yourself individually.**

Mirrors never lie. There is no running from your personal realities and time-proven traits. Deceiving others is relatively simple. Deceiving yourself is inordinately impossible. When you try to deceive yourself into thinking you're someone or something that you're not, it never ends well. You can become your very own worst enemy with self-deception that ultimately helps build those internal barriers you create to postpone and procrastinate action as well as derail you from your proposed sprint on the gun lap.

There has never been a substitute for honesty. Consider that many of us have said **the best time to start a diet is on a Monday or the first of the month.** Some think (and procrastinate) bigger and avoid starting that diet until the first of a new year. Why can't you start a major change in your life midafternoon on a Wednesday? When you try to deceive yourself as to who you are and what you truly will do, you become your own enemy. Consider Walt Kelly's words from his classic 1960s cartoon strip, *Pogo*: **"We have met the enemy and he is us."**

If, over the years, you've talked a lot about learning how to play a musical instrument, then come to grips with yourself. Are you really in a place in your life where you have the time for lessons and dedicated practicing? Is it still important to you now? Are there other bucket list items, desires, and aspirations that are more important? This is a time for deep personal reflection. It's surely the time to go back to the mirror for answers.

I have found a pragmatic, systemic approach to making important life (and gun-lap) decisions is best. Here are some things you might consider when defining your who, what, and where so you can make the best decisions while you attack new opportunities.

- Do an emotional download. Forget what you think about moving toward a new activity or objective. **Focus more on how you feel.**

- Clearly define your own expectations. What do you **really** want (and need) to get out of the new you?

- **Don't ask anyone for help.** This is all about you and needs to be your decision. It's nobody's business whether you should take piano lessons, learn to play golf, strive to run a marathon, or change your profession. People will always counsel you through their lens. This isn't a collaborative decision.

- Understand that **life decisions cost us something.** Whether it's time, money, or other personal resources, growing forward always comes with a cost.

- If you find that you've made a decision but keep postponing taking action on it, then it's more than likely you've made the wrong decision.

- Try hard to **whittle your life choices down to two options.** The more choices you have, the longer it will take you to make a decision and the more likely the process will become confusing and frustrating.

- I've found that if you pretend you're advising a relative or friend on the decision you're trying to make, you'll likely come up with new thoughts that will profoundly open your eyes to the logical conclusion. **Be a consultant to yourself.**

- **Be a contrarian to yourself.** Don't spend all your time focusing on all the reasons why you should learn to play golf, start painting with oils, enroll in a language class, take an exotic trip, or start volunteering in the community. Also spend time focusing on all the reasons why you shouldn't do something. This will help put the decision in perspective.

Sometimes where you are physically, mentally, even financially can be a deciding factor toward helping you conclude what's next for you in your life and whether certain gun-lap activities fit you. As obvious as these examples are, they demonstrate the kinds of scenarios one might face in decision-making. You wouldn't decide to become a long-distance runner if you suffer from a breathing problem. You likely wouldn't learn to play the piano if you are plagued with rheumatoid arthritis. You probably wouldn't pursue playing golf if you don't have the financial wherewithal to join a country club or pay for public course fees. You might not want to travel abroad extensively if you recently lost your spouse and had no one to join you. You likely wouldn't start a new business if you were on a modest fixed income. And on and on.

The message is simply to do a long, hard personal audit that should include thoughts about your time, your health, and your resources. Your conclusions will help you identify, qualify, and ultimately define what's next for you, and **there is always a *what's next for you*.** Take a thoughtful approach, and you'll find it.

The wonderful thing about life is that it's filled with opportunities and a huge range of choices. Whether it's business, recreation, sport, education, music, or art, looking toward new frontiers, new skills, new activities, new challenges, and new opportunities is a simple process. It's simply about work—putting the time into learning about the options, deep diving into each for better understanding, and making a decision (or decisions).

Sometimes, preconceived notions can get in the way. We've all heard about people who claimed to be tone-deaf and one day fell in love with singing in the church choir, loving every minute and note of it. There are people convinced they won't enjoy golf or tennis or bridge who then try the activity and become committed players.

As a collegiate and competitive athlete in my youth, a few knee surgeries, two hip replacements, and a fully replaced shoulder slowed down my vigorous exercise lifestyle dramatically. So upset about not being able to run a few miles daily or work out aggressively at a gym, I reluctantly let my wife convince me I should try power walking. Although I hated the notion of walking, in over three decades of marriage she's rarely been wrong, and I started walking (with her) in our hilly Atlanta neighborhood. I quickly realized it was challenging. It was vigorous. I even sweat and had sore muscles. In fact, I fell in love with long-distance walking and hiking, and wow, was I wrong. Yes, my beloved Kim was right again.

I was initially closed-minded. Don't be. Remember the old adage, **"The mind is like a parachute. It only works when it's open."**

CHAPTER FOUR

Dream a Little Dream

 *May sweet dreams be yours.*

Walt Disney said, "All our dreams can come true, if we have the courage to pursue them."

Success is all about the courage of conviction. This is especially true when you decide to sprint on the gun lap. **Conviction (belief), coupled with courage, confidence, aspiration, and passion are the ingredients necessary for a fully baked plan to rise and prosper.** Henry David Thoreau, the American author of *Walden* and other books, said, "I learned this, at least, by my experiment: that if one advances confidently in the direction of his dreams, and endeavors to live the life which he has imagined, he will meet with a success unexpected in common hours."

Why is it so important to have dreams? Why is it important to follow your dreams?

- As you grow older, dreams are even more important inasmuch as without dreams and aspirations, **you can quickly move from hopeful to hopeless.** Without dreams, you have little to live for.

- **Dreams keep you young.** They provide motivation to think and act for tomorrow and the future. Dreams bring forth optimism.

- As a child and young adult, you chased dreams constantly and viewed them as wishful thinking, enchanting, mystical, and magical. Now, with more maturity, **you have the benefit and wisdom to selectively choose those realistic dreams** that make sense and have personal relevancy.

- **Your dreams are exclusively owned by you.** You have the pride of ownership, and if your dreams are realized, you also have the power of accomplishment.

- **Dreams have no limits.** After all, there is only one rule in life, and that one rule is there are no rules! Don't forget you created your dreams. They operate under your rules.

- There is **nothing sweeter than seeing a dream come true.** Regardless of how massive or minute, the realization of a dream is absolute bliss.

Once you've decided your newfound gun-lap objectives, it's vital to dream about your endgame. Beginning with the end in mind through creative visualization can be incredibly beneficial in building your plan. Creative visualization is the cognitive process of purposefully generating visual mental images, with your eyes open or closed, and working to visualize what something will look like at the end of an endeavor.

It's the golfer who stares at his ball on the green before ever pulling his putter out of the bag, then mentally visualizes softly stroking the ball as it rolls straight into the cup. In his mind, he might also hear the ball drop into the hole, *ka-plink*.

Creatively visualizing what a dream, hope, or aspiration might look like once you complete the activity helps you dive into the process. For instance, if your bucket list objective is to be able to play children's songs for your grandchildren on the piano, closing your eyes and visualizing the children joyfully sitting around the piano wide-eyed and excited as a grandparent showcases skills to their delight mentally moves the activity from a dream closer to reality. Once you visualize something and emotionally feel what the endeavor would be like at successful conclusion, it provides motivation that will likely lead you to focus and work.

All three of my sons played college basketball. When my youngest son, Ryan, was a high-scoring shooting guard on his high school team, he suffered from poor performance on the foul line. Although he would score shot after shot on the court, when he was fouled, he was very inefficient at shooting foul shots. He met with a friend of mine, Dr. Jack Llewellyn, a prominent sports psychologist. He told Ryan, **"If you go out on your driveway every day and take fifty slow, form-perfect foul shots a day, you'll dramatically improve your foul shooting percentage."**

Ryan was confused and replied, "Dr. Jack, I do that now. In fact, I probably shoot one hundred foul shots a day, but my shooting percentage is not growing."

Jack surprisingly responded with, "Ryan, what I want you to do differently is take those fifty-plus perfect shots every day without the ball. Yes, shoot without the ball, and visualize the perfect shot going in the goal shot after shot after shot."

So Ryan went out every day and creatively visualized his shot and saw the imaginary ball go in the basket shot after shot after shot. The funny thing about it was that my next door neighbor called me one evening and said to me, "Ira, I've watched Ryan practice basketball in your driveway day after day. You, my friend, are a real cheapskate. **Get him a ball**. The poor kid is practicing without a ball. If you can't afford one, I'll get him a present!"

The remark was funny, but Ryan's success on the foul line in high school and later in college became historic, breaking his own college foul-shooting record twice and, at one point, leading the NCAA in foul-shooting percentage. It all came about through visualizing his goal.

You too need to **define your objective and visualize every step** needed to successfully complete the task at hand.

The wonderful thing about pursuing the gun-lap opportunity and working toward a new project, skill, endeavor, or activity is the new learning you'll be gaining. After all, **when you're through learning, you're through!**

You were deceived when you were in school. Some teacher or professor likely said to you, "Success is in the hands of the learned." Not so. Not true. In reality, **success is actually in the hands of the *learning*.** It's a continuous process. Racing on the gun lap provides the opportunity for continuous learning and improvement. Now that's exciting. That's happy talk!

CHAPTER FIVE

The Fountain of Youth

➡️ *Find joy in your work, and you'll discover the fountain of youth.*

Famous actress Sophia Loren wrote, "There is a fountain of youth. It is your mind, your talents, the creativity you bring to your life and the lives of people you love. When you learn to tap this source, you will truly have defeated age."

Only the young at heart can run the gun lap. *Youth* is a relative term. I don't mean chronological youth. I mean

staying young in your heart and your head. **Youth is all about being open-minded, taking risks, and embracing change.** This kind of youthful thinking can come at any age and at any stage of your life.

We all know seventy-five-year-olds who are open-minded, energetic, highly inquisitive, adventurous, optimistic, spirited, and passionate about all they do and everything around them. Sadly, we also know twenty-five-year-olds who are closed-minded, pessimistic, cautious, lethargic, and have no passion for anything or anybody.

Consider that children who color outside the lines, invent games, and invent rules to those games are happy as a lark. Unfortunately, **we card-carrying adults are typically reserved and reluctant.** We oftentimes meet change and challenge in a highly conservative, hesitant manner. Rather than emulating young people and embracing their willingness to create, invent, aspire, and make new efforts and figuring out how we can adapt new thinking in sync with our time-tested wisdom, we criticize. Deep down inside, we know that happiness is directly correlative to being young at heart and young in mind. However, we'd prefer to avoid change, and instead of meeting it with energy and gusto, we typically sit back and bemoan the new order with a package vanilla phrase: **"This is not the way we've always done it."**

There are only three things you can do when confronted with change. You can:

1   Ignore it.

2   Adapt and adjust to it.

3   Make additional changes.

You will never drink an ounce of the fountain of youth if you take the "ignore it" route. Ignore change, and you will evaporate. **It won't happen here always happens here.** The unsinkable (*Titanic*) sunk. The unbelievable (transplanting a human heart) is now believable. The incredible (creating life in a test tube) is now credible. The indestructible (the Holy Roman Empire) was destroyed. The unbeatable (Nazi Germany) was beaten. The unthinkable (cloning a sheep) is now thinkable.

IRA BLUMENTHAL

Change is inevitable. Growth is optional.

If you just want to survive in your quest for the next step, next chapter, and gun lap in your life, adapting and adjusting to change will help you tread water, survive, endure, subsist, and continue on. There's something about just surviving and enduring that doesn't excite me, and I'm certain it's not exciting to you.

Adapting and adjusting is simply rolling with the punches, letting the tide take you in and out whenever and wherever it chooses to flow. With this strategy, you lose control and will likely never achieve your objectives. Still, many of us would prefer riding the tide, not bucking the system, and adapting to the changes around us. If that's your choice, fine. Best of luck living a world of stuff versus substance.

But if you're truly gearing up to sprint on whatever gun lap you've chosen to race (i.e., education, art, science, enterprise, fitness, travel, adventure, etc.), the final choice related to change is for you.

Yes, **making other changes in your life is the key to facing the changes all around you.** Be a change master. Be a change catalyst. Invent, create, reach, do, aspire, seek, and pursue everything and anything new for you.

Walk differently. Talk differently. Embrace a new style or fashion. Read books you've always wanted to read. Travel to places you've always dreamed of visiting. Learn a new language or how to master functions on a computer. Raise the bar on your exercise regimen. Start a new business. Mentor someone. Volunteer for a cause you've always wanted to help. Paint your first painting or build your first treehouse or learn to play the guitar. Coach Little League baseball or soccer. Help out at cheerleading practice. Plant a vegetable garden.

Make other changes!

Making other changes and trying new things (or returning to the things you've done and left behind many years ago) will help you grow, thrive, and prosper personally. **Take the attitude that some of the best years of your life are yet to come.**

Want to stay young and drink from the fountain of youth? Consider these pearls of wisdom.

- Don't ever save anything, ever, for the future or for that special occasion. **Every day of your life is a special occasion.** Use each today to the fullest. Don't hold back, hesitate, or delay. It's a basketball phrase but works on the gun lap, namely, **"You cannot score unless you shoot."**

- *Now* is an important word for everyone on the gun lap. It's a word missing from the U.S. Declaration of Independence, which provides us the "unalienable rights" of "life, liberty, and the pursuit of happiness." To all energetic, spirited people (on the gun lap for certain), it should read we are entitled to **"life, liberty, and the pursuit of happiness—now!"**

- **Never forget you have endless possibilities.** Within realistic reason, you can do whatever you want to do, be whatever you want to be, and accomplish anything you want to accomplish.

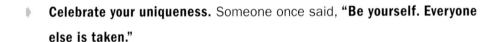

- **Celebrate your uniqueness.** Someone once said, **"Be yourself. Everyone else is taken."**

- Try a few new procedures and practices in your life. Switch sides of the bed with your partner, brush your teeth with your nondominant hand, put the mouse on the other side of the computer, or try buttoning your shirt one-handed. These little self-inflicted changes help work unused parts of your brain. Another way to go (and grow) is to do a few common things blindfolded or with your eyes shut. If you get up in the middle of the night,

navigate to the bathroom (or the refrigerator) with your eyes closed. Sort coins with your eyes closed. **Challenge yourself to grow, and you will.**

▶ **Use your brain.** It sounds silly, but the reservoir filling the fountain of youth is your brain. Keep thinking. Attack problems, debate issues, memorize poetry (just like when you were a school child), or provide yourself your own unique brain teasers (i.e., try to list the names of one hundred friends from your entire life; try to list the names of fifty movies you've seen over the years; try to list the names of fifty classic songs

you loved to sing). Use your brain. Avoid mindless activities. Only watch television to be entertained at times and to be educated often.

▶ **Think young.** Within realistic reason, act young. Be young. Mark Twain wrote, "Life would be infinitely happier if we could only be born at the age of eighty and gradually approach eighteen."

▶ **Don't leave a trail of regrets.** You'll regret the things you haven't done much more than those you have done.

You can't find, much less drink from, the fountain of youth if you don't take the attitude that you can, in fact, be young (in mind, in spirit, in heart) forever. **After all, an important key to successful aging is to avoid thinking about aging.** Oliver Wendell Holmes Jr. said, "To be seventy years young is sometimes far more cheerful and hopeful than to be forty years old."

CHAPTER SIX

The Commitment.
The Plan.

➡ *Make the commitment.*
Craft the plan.

Existential philosopher Jean-Paul Sartre wrote,
"Commitment is an act, not a word." There can be no
success, no accomplishment, and no achievement on
the gun lap if you are not fully vested and committed
to the task at hand. Although you need to be flexible in
your approaches to fulfill various commitments, it's still
an undeniable fact that having no commitment leads you
to having no attainment.

Passion is surely a part of the process. Physicist Albert Einstein said, "I have no special talents. I am only passionately curious." When you make the giant step to learn something new, try something new, be something new, and sprint on the gun lap, **passion is always the driving force that leads to commitment**. If you want something badly enough and accept that hard work, diligence, focus, and a major commitment (time, resources, energy, etc.) is necessary to achieve success, you will be on the first rung of the ladder climbing to fulfill your goals.

There will be bumps in the road. There will be setbacks. There will be self-doubt. There will be questions. It has been said that a bend in the road is not the end of the road. Oftentimes, what seems to be a stumbling block could actually be a stepping stone if you're willing to learn from it and grow from it. However, **slight detours and diversions should not deter you from your vision, mission, and, most importantly, your commitment to succeed.**

There are three keys to building a commitment to succeed on the gun lap, namely, uncompromising sacrifice, crystal-clear purpose, and unwavering determination.

First, let us explore **uncompromising sacrifice.** In order for you to finish well on the gun lap and achieve new or renewed goals, you will have to give something up, trade something down, make an investment (time, energy, money, resources), and define a new priority. If your bucket list aspiration is to learn to play golf and eventually be a 15-handicap player, then you'll need to devote the time, energy, and resources to achieve that gun-lap goal. **Success and ascending any summit and achieving any goal are deliberate**. After all, the person on top of a mountain peak didn't fall there. It was by design. It was by plan. It was deliberate, and it was, typically, through great sacrifice. Lukewarm hearts can't achieve great accomplishments. Knowing full well that a gun-lap sacrifice might challenge other life (and family) activities, uncompromising sacrifices aren't always easy, but **if you're willing to compromise your current state of affairs and interrupt the norm and perhaps move in what could be an uncomfortable space in favor of your important quest, success will surely and ultimately be yours.**

Secondly, **there can be no commitment if you don't first have a crystal-clear purpose behind the activity and endeavor you are pursuing. With purpose comes power.** Purpose, in short, is tightly attached to direction. When thinking about your purpose and charting your direction, ask yourself the following questions.

- **How will I define success?**
- **Why is this important to me?**
- **Does this light my fire and excite me?**
- **What is my destination?**
- **Which way should I be heading?**
- **What is my contingency plan if course correction is needed?**
- **How will I know when I reach journey's end?**

Finally, let's address the compelling imperative defined as **unwavering determination.** It is a fact of life **that determined people blend a mixture of commitment and purpose in order to succeed.** I've found that the difference between significant, accomplished individuals and those who are less than accomplished and often less significant is the level of determination. Failures are usually defined by lack of determination.

Determined people abhor the word *can't* and never see failure as an option. Iconic basketball star Michael Jordan once said in an interview, "Obstacles don't have to stop you. If you run into a wall, don't turn around and give up. Figure out how to climb it, go through it, or work around it. Hard work is the answer."

Determination is usually accompanied by optimism. There's a fantastic story about Thomas Alva Edison being interviewed by a newspaper man who asked, "Mr. Edison, I understand it took you nearly 10,000 tries to invent the lightbulb. What did you learn through all those failures?" Edison coyly responded, "Sir, I learned 9,999 ways not to invent a lightbulb."

You must be resolute in your gun-lap efforts. Either find a way or create a way. There is no place for turning back and giving up.

I'd be remiss if I didn't share with you one of my favorite quotations. Reverend Theodore Munger said, "Nothing in the world can take the place of persistence. Talent will not; nothing is more common than unsuccessful men with talent. Genius will not; unrewarded genius is almost a proverb. Education alone will not; the world is full of educated derelicts. Persistence and determination alone are omnipotent. The slogan 'press on' has solved and always will solve the problems of the human race."

It takes courage to face the challenges, make the choices, and even face the uncertainty that comes with your commitment to a purpose. Action is the key. Remember what Sartre wrote: **"Commitment is an act, not a word."** There will be setbacks, resistance, and sometimes doubt, but focusing on your endgame and the energy generated by the gun lap will get you through.

Once the commitment is in place and the purpose as well as the supporting determination are aligned, it's time to define your gun-lap plan for execution. I have found that if you chart a plan similar to ways corporations attempt to accomplish their objectives, it's easier to understand, quantify, and track. Taking an altered business plan format, with a few simplified adjustments, you should define and write down the following three simple steps for your gun-lap plan.

1 **VISION:** Define what you desire to achieve or experience. Take a little time to imagine your endgame. As referenced earlier, creatively visualize what accomplishing this vision will look and feel like. An example could be "My vision is to be able to sit around the campfire on the beach this summer at our annual family vacation and play five sing-along songs on the guitar for my grandchildren."

2   **OBJECTIVES:** Define a manageable list of objectives so that you can fulfill your vision. Build in thoughts about the barriers to achieving your objectives and course correction if your plan doesn't go exactly as you hoped. An example could be "My objectives are to learn to play the guitar, master a basic chord progression, and proficiently learn how to play five children's songs by the Fourth of July."

3   **COMMITMENT:** Fully define exactly what you need to do to move your concept to completion, step by step. Specify your time line as well. Continuing the example: "After buying a beginner's guitar, I will take eight lessons in April and May so I can master the standard G, C, and D chord progression. I will work on five children's songs and practice them thirty minutes four nights a week in the month of June so I can be ready for debut Fourth of July weekend."

Of course, this is a simplified, almost obvious plan, but **typically, if you fully define a gun-lap plan on paper for continuous review, the task becomes that much more important, defined, and accomplished.**

Commit to your plan, supported by a strong personal purpose and passion, add some solid determination, and bring it all together in a focused written document for reminder and review. Back to Thoreau for inspirational words: **"Go confidently in your dreams. Live the life you've imagined."**

CHAPTER SEVEN

The Extra Mile Is Never Crowded

 *Strive to be extraordinary.*

It's been said that "the difference between ordinary and extraordinary is simply a little extra." Too many people talk a good game, think a great game, and sit back and let the world pass them by. It's the extraordinary person who is never satisfied and is constantly striving for yet another conquest.

The entire context of the gun lap is based on the reality

that everything in life, including life itself, has a time limit. High school lasts for four years and it's over. College ends with a graduation. Many jobs have a time line or, in retail terms, a shelf life. Relationships come and go, as do careers. If you accept the reality that life is all about time lines and time limits, it seems obvious you should strive to make the most of the time you have on this planet. The gun lap is truly **a wake-up call designed to make you focus on all you have yet to accomplish and experience. The only thing sadder than unfinished business is, perhaps, business never started.**

Ordinary people live contented lives where *good enough* is fine.

Extraordinary people committed to living life to its fullest take a contrary view and say, **"Good enough never is."**

Think hard about your dreams and your hopes. If what you dreamed about and hoped for back in your teens and perhaps even your twenties has not come to fruition, then your daily question to yourself should be **"If not now, when?"**

The AARP, America's largest public organization, with over thirty-eight million members, actively promotes the reality that "aging is changing." In fact, one can join the AARP when they reach the ripe young age of fifty. Supporting the position that "it's never too late" and that "old can be bold," the *RP* in *AARP* now stands for real possibilities. I love that. You should love and embrace that too.

In its *AARP Bulletin* and *AARP The Magazine*, they constantly showcase stories of people over the age of fifty who dared and cared to move from ordinary to extraordinary as they raced the extra mile on the gun lap. These real people pursuing real possibilities include both those who had bucket-list objectives as well as those who simply pursued a great second career. Although the following examples seem unusual and unique, they aren't. They simply represent real people (names were withheld on purpose) who are striving for continuous improvement, unending education, new challenges, new opportunities, and a focus on life fulfillment. They all obviously embrace real possibilities.

Consider these real second career stories:

- A seventy-year-old man became a sailboat captain.

- A sixty-eight-year-old woman started a dog-walking company.

- A sixty-three-year-old man went to nursing school.

- A fifty-eight-year-old woman became a flight attendant.

- A sixty-seven-year-old man became a certified personal trainer.

- A sixty-eight-year-old woman became a U.S. park ranger.

- A seventy-year-old man became a museum president.

Consider these real bucket list stories:

- A seventy-eight-year-old woman learned to be a metal sculptor.

- A ninety-one-year-old woman started taking modern dance.

- A fifty-six-year-old woman ran her first marathon.

- A sixty-eight-year-old woman wrote and produced her first play.

- A fifty-five-year-old man became a skydiver.

- A fifty-nine-year-old man learned how to play the trumpet.

- A fifty-six-year-old man became a magician.

The extraordinary choose to live their lives to the fullest. Every morning, you can choose how you'll spend your day. You can choose joy, happiness, helpfulness, energy, spirit, kindness, philanthropy, learning, working, seeking, experimenting, and more. You can also choose sadness, depression, helplessness, pessimism, laziness, sarcasm, boredom, and more. **To feel the freedom that comes from being able to do new things and accomplish new goals is wonderful and magical. Even having the ability to make new mistakes is energizing. Life is for the living.**

The late Steve Jobs said, "Your time is limited, so don't waste it living someone else's life. Don't be trapped by dogma—which is living with the results of other people's thinking. Don't let the noise of others' opinions drown out your own inner voice. And most important, have the courage to follow your heart and intuition. They somehow already know what you truly want to become."

It's a sad but true fact that years, perhaps decades, from now, you **will be more disappointed by all the opportunities you didn't take and all the things you avoided doing than by the ones that you decided to do. It's never too late to do, to try, to aspire, to achieve, to grow.** You may very well be the only person in your family or in your circle of friends raising the bar and actively pursuing your dreams on the gun lap. That's okay. The extra mile is never crowded.

Life, after all, is a series of second chances, comebacks, and do-overs. Racing on the gun lap, you could, for the first time in your life, be the person you've always wanted to be and do things you've only dreamed about. Again, if not now, when? What's also terrific is that as you grow older, it is often easier to be positive. You care less about what others think, because you've gained both a sense of perspective and wisdom.

There was a time when you were younger when your mindset was focused on strong beliefs. In other words, you believed this would happen, and you believed that would happen. You might not have been sure, but you still had beliefs. You're now approaching an age of certainty. Whereas believing is conditional and speculative, you have now evolved to a time where you no longer believe inasmuch as your age, maturity, experience, and wisdom (*wisdom*...what a marvelous word) moves your thinking from conditional and speculative to certainty. You, therefore, are moving from believing to knowing. Yes, you now know something will happen, not just believe it will happen.

That helps you make even better decisions on the gun lap.

Country singer and actress Reba McEntire shared her thoughts about aging and success when she said, "To succeed in life, you need three things: a wishbone, a backbone, and a funny bone." It's the wishbone that is vital for all gun-lap competitors.

As you grow older, continue to grow wiser. Avoid meaningless "time vampires" that waste your valuable, precious time. You're not old. Look at it as you've just been young for a very long time!

Avoid doing nothing. Do something that's important to you. Speaking of doing nothing, I'm reminded of an old joke. A woman asked her husband, "What are you going to do today?" He said, "Nothing." She said, "Honey, you did that yesterday." He said, "I wasn't finished."

You are not finished. The old adage "today is the first day of the rest of your life" applies here. Strive for extraordinary!

CHAPTER EIGHT

Celebrating Success

➤ *Celebrate and share your success.*

Where you start is not nearly as important as where you finish. But by the same token, why you started the journey in the first place is just as important as how you accomplished your goal.

First and foremost, **you don't have to wait until you cross the finish line to feel proud of your accomplishment. Be proud of yourself with every step you take to get**

there. Booker T. Washington wrote, "I have learned that success is to be measured not so much by the position that one has reached in life as by the obstacles which he has overcome while trying to succeed."

It's only natural to question the decision to embark upon any journey, and self-doubt is a natural phenomenon that you may very well have faced. However, the joy of finishing—in some cases, not finishing but actively pursuing—is always well worth any angst you might have experienced. A hugely profound thought comes from a poem by Edgar A. Guest, first published in 1920: "There's no thrill in easy sailing when the skies are clear and blue. There's no joy in merely doing things which any one can do. But there is some satisfaction that is mighty sweet to take, when you reach a destination that you never thought you'd make."

It's a valuable exercise to review the game films, so to speak, after you have accomplished your gun-lap objectives. **Review the journey step by step, point by point, play by play.** The objective is twofold. On one hand, you want to embed in your mind all the things you did along the way that worked, proved fruitful, and led you to your success. On the other hand, you also want to remind yourself and focus on all the challenges you faced that perhaps could have been handled differently (or better). **Obsess with continuous improvement.** Noted author William Faulkner said, "Always dream and shoot higher than you know you can do. Do not bother just to be better than your contemporaries or predecessors. Try to be better than yourself."

Some people prefer to celebrate success quietly, under the radar screen and alone. Others can't wait to share and get the proverbial high five. From my experience, here are a handful of ways you might consider celebrating your gun-lap success.

▶   Kick back, take a deep breath, and savor the moment.

- Share the news with those you love and respect. Don't waste the news on those who are marginal in your life. There's an important saying worthy of consideration: "Never make someone a priority when all you are to them is an option."

- Be humble as the accolades come your way.

- Do something you hardly had time to do (and enjoy) while you were sprinting on the gun lap. You sacrificed something while running the race. Indulge yourself now.

- Take a day off before you work on your next gun-lap goal.

- Support someone else who is on a similar gun-lap quest.

- Journal and document the details (and the emotions) of your journey. It's all very likely a memory you want to save and savor.

In the marble rotunda lobby of the world headquarters of The Coca-Cola Company, there is a bust of one of the legendary former leaders of Coca-Cola, Robert Woodruff. Above his statue, there is a plaque that gives his life's creed: "There is no limit to what man can do or how far he can go if he doesn't care who gets the credit." Although you should be very proud of what you've accomplished while running hard on your very own gun lap, your point of success should also be marked with sharing the credit with those around you who supported your effort and made their own sacrifices to ensure you could accomplish your goals. Think about the resources you allocated, the time you put into the quest, and the myopic focus you put forth, then also think about it in terms of what others had to endure supporting you. **It's amazing how far a sincere thank you goes.**

One of my favorite all-time songs is "The Wind Beneath My Wings," made famous by singer Bette Midler, written by Jeff Silbar and Larry Henley. Its powerful words remind us to take the time and thank those who have been our source for wind that helped us rise, soar, and succeed.

We very often get so caught up in and distracted by our own quests, our own objectives, our own destinations, that we sometimes forget to show appreciation to those along the way who helped us on our journey. **As committed as we have been to our objectives is as committed as we should be to those who helped and supported us.**

CHAPTER NINE

What's Next?

➡️ *There's something exciting about a tomorrow.*

It's an amazing, wonderful, optimistic, important thought that some of the best days of our lives haven't happened yet. We've all heard the wonderful words from the Broadway hit *Annie* that proudly proclaim, "The sun will come out tomorrow. Bet your bottom dollar that tomorrow, there'll be sun."

Whether you accomplished your gun-lap endeavor or just finished well (and finishing well is something to be

proud of), it's now time to do it all again. Every day provides you the opportunity to do it again but, more importantly, do it again using the patterns that previously proved successful or the lessons you hopefully learned from past failures. **Success typically breeds additional success if you repeat the pattern, emulate the model, and remember the steps you took in the journey.** By the same token, failure is just as important inasmuch as it should teach us what not to do again and how to do it all differently next chance.

My wife, Kim, and I constantly tell our children (and now our grandchildren) **"We pray you make new mistakes!"** Every one of us makes mistakes. The key is not to dwell on the mistake but to learn from it and avoid making the same ones again. After all, isn't insanity doing the same thing over and over again and expecting different results?

You've completed a gun-lap journey. You sprinted hard for the finish line, and you completed this particular endeavor, quest, and race. You should be proud of yourself for finishing well, proud of yourself for finishing. It's less about the victory or the medal and more about the personal pride, hopefully great pride, in finishing. A dear friend of mine, singer, songwriter, author, and motivational speaker Tom Sullivan defines pride in a meaningful way.

P	Personal
R	Responsibility for
I	Individual
D	Daily
E	Effort

Yes, we each must be **personally responsible for our individual daily efforts** in all we do. That **personal responsibility** should logically lead us to the conclusion that one or two or even three races on the gun lap are not necessarily enough. What's next? Goal-oriented people seeking life fulfillment focus on their current efforts and endeavors but concurrently give some thought about the next venture (adventure, perhaps).

A simple yet pragmatic pattern of activities can help you decide what's next and what new (or renewed) gun-lap race you're destined to run as your sequel.

1 Singer Jimmy Buffett talks about clearing one's head with "mental floss." Clear your head. Take a walk, run a mile, go biking, go hiking, or do whatever you love to do that is mindless and provides you time to just plain think. **Clear your head!**

2 **Draft a list of alternatives.** From the ridiculous to the sublime, write that list with energy, reckless abandon, and spirit. Remember you'll eventually be rereading and reviewing the list, eliminating options until you're down to a handful of real choices (ideally two).

3 **Edit, edit, and reedit your list.** Eliminate the absurd items. Eliminate the unrealistic items. Eliminate those items that are just not threshold activities and simply "nice to do" items. After all, many things in life will catch your eye but only a few will catch your heart. **Through a process of elimination, pare down your list to only those realistic, relevant activities that truly catch your heart.**

4 **Pre-search and research like crazy.** In business, we call this due diligence. **Study everything about the activity and goal you're potentially**

pursuing. What is the investment necessary? How will it change and challenge your life and status quo? Is it realistic for you? Is it something you can be passionate about? Is it something you've dreamed about doing for years? Pile up and organize the data. Yes, your lists might have lists, but that's okay. After all, this is another important life decision.

5 Once you've made fact-based decisions based on your personal research and whittled down your list to a few (again, try getting to two) alternatives, **it's now time for validation.** Remember, you often don't know what you don't know. Validation is as simple as finding others who attacked the very same goals, aspirations, and activities you're considering going after. Shadow them and perhaps observe what they've done, what they're doing, and most importantly, how they're doing it (whatever "it" might be). Things aren't always what they seem. **That's why validation is vital!**

6 **It's now time to clear your head a second time and be very thoughtful.** After all, you're about to go through the process of commitment again. Think hard. In the words of the late, legendary women's basketball coach Pat Summitt, "Left foot, right foot, breathe." **Take a thoughtful step-by-step approach, with deep breathing, thinking, perhaps even meditation, and make your decision.**

7 To use a common term on movie sets, **"Lights, camera, action!"** Yes, it's time for action. Strap on your running shoes, stretch a bit, and start your next step race, focusing on yet another gun lap.

The great news about seeking next steps when you are focused on continuous improvement as well as raising the bar on life's experiences, endeavors, and even enterprises is that **the choices are never-ending**. If you are seeking a new or second career or are starting a new business venture, those endless choices are more in line with personal skill sets, interests, financial status, education, personal network, opportunities, and more. On the other hand, **when you are considering what has been aptly called a bucket list opportunity, those choices are as wide and deep as the Atlantic Ocean.**

To provide a little bit of assistance, here's a short ABCD list of thought start-ers to consider. Some of these items might fit your personal to-do list, and others just might not be relevant. Nonetheless, it's meant to provide you a top-line list designed to get you thinking and, ultimately, doing. I've provided examples up through **D, which clearly stands for "Do something!"**

ATTEND

...an event you've never attended (i.e., NCAA Final Four, the Masters, an opera, an air show, etc.).

...a speakers series to expand your knowledge base.

...a fitness class and commit to healthy exercise.

...a special event or festival you've never experienced.

...a cooking or dance or art class.

BECOME

...certified in CPR.

...a Boy Scout leader.

...a public servant and run for office.

...a foster parent.

...ambidextrous.

...a youth athletic referee or umpire.

...a committee leader in a civic organization.

CHANGE

...a habit you've been trying to break for years.

...your dining-out pattern and learn to cook.

...your fear of something and take a chance.

...your reluctance to be an activist for a cause and then act.

...your hesitancy to speak in public and work on that skill.

...your recreational pursuits and embrace a new hobby.

DO SOMETHING, LIKE

...learn to dance.

...learn a new language.

...travel to your dream destination.

...hike the Appalachian Trail.

...improve your golf game.

...take painting lessons.

Needless to say, you could put lists on top of lists. What should be obvious is that **your choices are never-ending, and they are your choices**. The good news is opportunities designed to help you rise, thrive, and experience are great. The bad news is that this wide range of opportunities will challenge you to make the right choice. The choice process can be filled with confusion, stress, and anxiety. Yet finding the single very best alternative activity for your next gun-lap race is all positive, all good, all productive, and the kind of challenge you should have more of. I say bring it on!

So what's next?

CONCLUSION

An Author's Confession

➡️ *I succeeded when I lost my excuses.*

As the father of five, the grandfather of seven, and one who has delivered over two thousand speeches on five continents, I probably should have told my kids, grandkids, and audiences, **"Do what I say, not what I do."**

We've all been there, done that, been there and done that again. We've all given sound advice, but hypocritical as we humans tend to be, we also pontificate, advise, counsel, and guide others in paths we suggest they travel yet often don't heed our own advice. It was precisely discovering the concept of the gun lap that made this author come to the conclusion that it was time to walk the talk, make strong resolutions, make new commitments, and, most importantly, complete the endeavor.

You see, I have been blessed. I have the marriage of marriages, an amazing array of children who are all well-adjusted solid citizens, and an enviable career as a consultant advising The Coca-Cola Company for nearly twenty-seven continuous years. I am an author and a public speaker who has opened for the likes of both President Bushes, General Colin Powell, Polish president Lech Walesa, Henry Kissinger, Cal Ripken Jr., Pakistani prime minister Benazir Bhutto, Russia's Mikhail Gorbachev, Baseball Hall of Famer Tommy

Lasorda, Senator Bob Dole, and more. I have partnered with iconic rock-and-roll star Steven Tyler, and we cocreated a national charity. I've worked with media mogul Ted Turner on a foundation. Today, I even serve as the CEO of the Pat Summitt Leadership Group, and I have been honored with awards and accolades and respected as an innovator through my historical work for companies such as McDonald's, Walmart, and others. I'm not boasting. I'm counting my blessings.

Of course, I'm proud of my life, humbled by accolades sent my way, and totally appreciative to all those who have helped me in my journey. Oh yes, there are so many people I'm indebted to who have made an indelible, positive mark on my life. Nonetheless, no different than you, dear reader, I have lists of unfinished business. There are so many things I've wanted to do, planned on doing, and still dream of accomplishing. However, as each year of my life passes, the list of unfulfilled New Year's resolutions grows painfully longer and longer.

For ten years, I resolved to learn the D chord on my guitar. Never did that. Never came close. Never tried. For at least two decades, I have had book project after book project sit in outline form in file folders marked *future*. They're still there. I had a bucket list objective to hike the Appalachian Trail. A few years back, Kim and I started the trail and hiked fifteen or so miles with a plan to continue the trail in small doses each year, and we haven't been back since. I planned on going back to my roots and continuing the piano lessons I took in high school. I bought a piano, talked the talk, but still haven't lifted a finger (literally and figuratively) to realize that aspiration. I wanted to author a book on my family's history. I have files of notes that have been sitting around for years. Oh yes, I planned to build a treehouse, write and produce a Broadway play, build a restaurant concept for healthy foods on college campuses, and on and on and on.

Sure, I'm proud of what I have accomplished in my life. But there needs to be more. Sitting down with a seventy-something friend who was planning on starting a new business, I told him **"Go for it. You're in your gun lap, and why not?"** He loved my term and shared his commitment to start the new enterprise. When he turned to me and asked me what about my gun lap, I paused. I thought for a few minutes, and I responded with **"You're right. If not now, when?"**

The next day, I formed a new business with my three sons, and we started dabbling in entrepreneurial ventures. I moved forward more aggressively trying to create my healthful restaurant concept. I became more focused on marketing the musical comedy my wife and I coauthored. (Broadway is our target, but we'll accept offers from any community theatre. Just give me a call.) I started two new books, one of which is the book you've just read. Kim and I do plan on getting back to the Appalachian Trail endeavor, and I now have no reluctance to start a new hobby or enterprise ever again.

I'm a believer. I'm totally focused on next steps!

I've made a commitment to focus the rest of my life, convinced it could become the best of my life, to finishing the unfinished.

What's important to note is that everything I consider, everything I do, and everything I aspire to become has absolutely nothing to do with money. It's all about fulfillment. It's all about personal pride in the quest. It's all about working hard to finish well.

I've seen the light. Procrastination is no longer one of my (sad) attributes. Hypocrisy is no longer one of my traits. Sure, I'm only human and will make mistakes (hopefully new mistakes), but I am more energized than ever before.

I hope to see you all racing on the gun lap. Don't lose sight of your dreams. Don't forget your hopes and aspirations.

If not now, when?

Acknowledgments

A BIG THANK YOU goes out to my personal editors and dear advisers, Kim, Eric, Jeffrey, and Ryan Blumenthal. I also appreciate the brilliant and profound people I've quoted throughout *Your Best Is Next*. From Mark Twain to Jean-Paul Sartre, from friend Steven Tyler to Albert Einstein and other visionaries quoted, their individual and collective inspiration fired my aspiration. I am also appreciative for my wonderful editor and friend Meg Gibbons of Simple Truths. I am thankful she believed in me. Finally, I also want to acknowledge Bill Burgess, who at ninety-one years young inspires me and continuously demonstrates the concept of young at heart.

About the Author

IRA BLUMENTHAL is a highly acclaimed business visionary, a best-selling author, a former university professor, a much sought-after public speaker who's delivered over two thousand speeches on five continents, a former Grand Masters World Cup athlete and collegiate coach, a globally respected business development and branding expert, a former lead consultant for The Coca-Cola Company (nearly twenty-seven years), and a former advisor to world-class companies such as McDonald's, Walmart, and Disney. He has successfully worked with media mogul Ted Turner, rock-and-roll icon Steven Tyler, and others. He sits on various boards (Blaze Sports, Janie's Fund, etc.) and serves as CEO of the Pat Summitt Leadership Group. Married to Kim for over thirty-five years, he has five children and seven grandchildren. Ira's most important guiding principle is that the two most important days in your life are the day you were born and the day you found out why. Ira Blumenthal found his why.